Explore Outer Space with Cosmic Chase

A story about outer space will always be a captivating and exciting experience for young children. There's something special about the solar system- planets, stars, rockets, and astronauts that encourage children's imaginations and allows them to dream big. "Explore Outer Space with Cosmic Chase" is a wonderful bedtime story that shares the adventure of a young astronaut who goes on an incredible journey into our fantastic universe. Your child will explore the galaxy with Cosmic Chase and learn so much about the world beyond our planet. This bedtime story will keep your little one looking forward to going to bed every night for an out-of-this-world adventure.

by Shelly and Joseph Rollins

MARS

EARTH

VENUS

MERCURY

SUN

There is a boy named Chase who loves to stare at the stars and moon.
Chase decided he would travel to outer space someday soon.
He made a list and packed the important items that could fit.
Then he put on his astronaut suit and took off in his rocketship.

JUPITER

SATURN

URANUS

NEPTUNE

Chase came upon the sun, which was much bigger than he realized.
The sun's rays were so powerful it made Chase squint his eyes.
The sun is special because it warms the universe and gives it light.
Without the sun as the biggest star, it would always be the night.

SUN

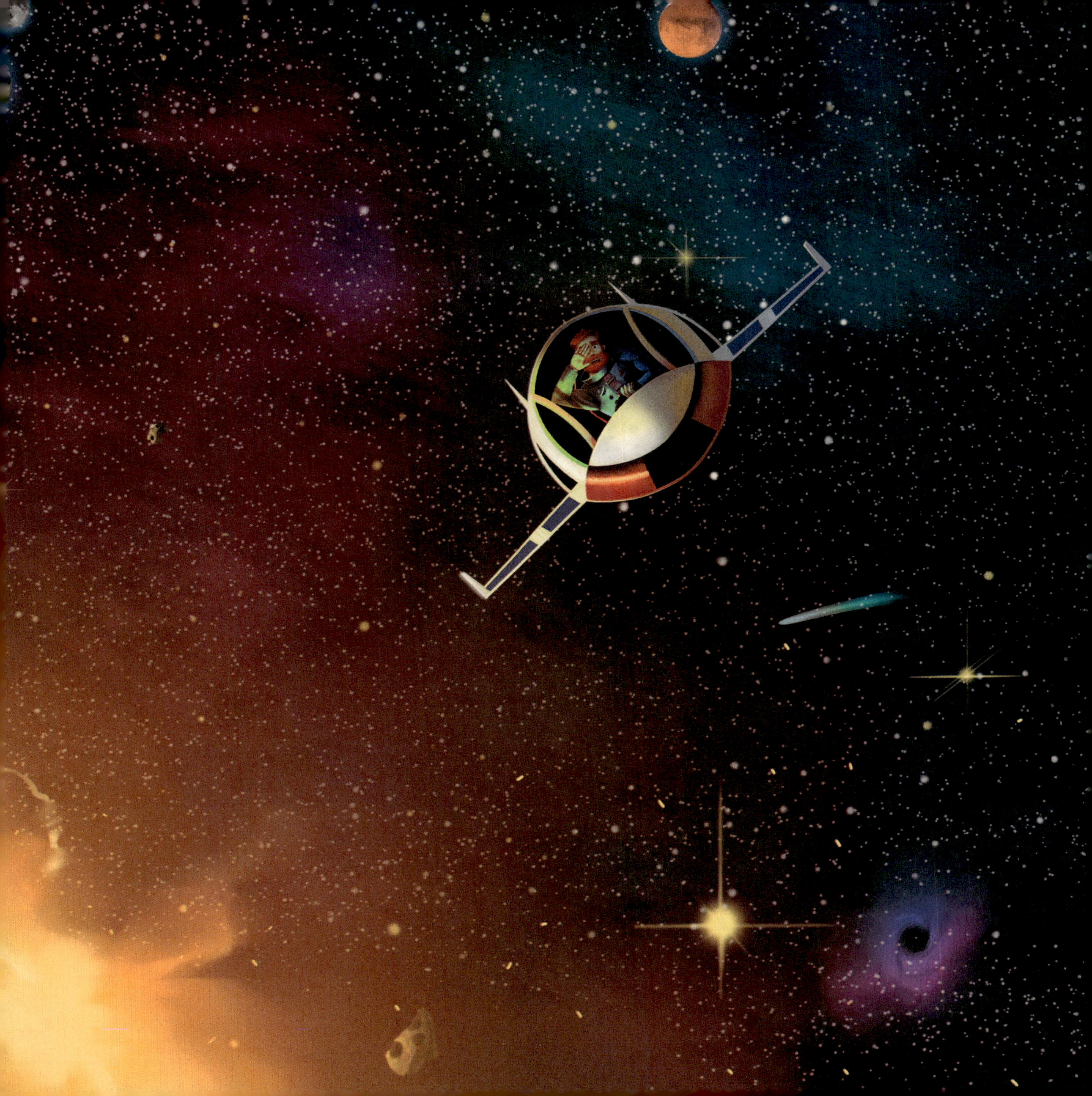

Next, Chase landed on Mercury, which is the closest planet to the sun.
Of all the planets in the solar system, Mercury is the smallest one.
Suddenly, an asteroid hit the planet, causing Chase and his rocket to shake.
Chase then took off in his rocketship to get away from Mercury's big quake.

MERCURY

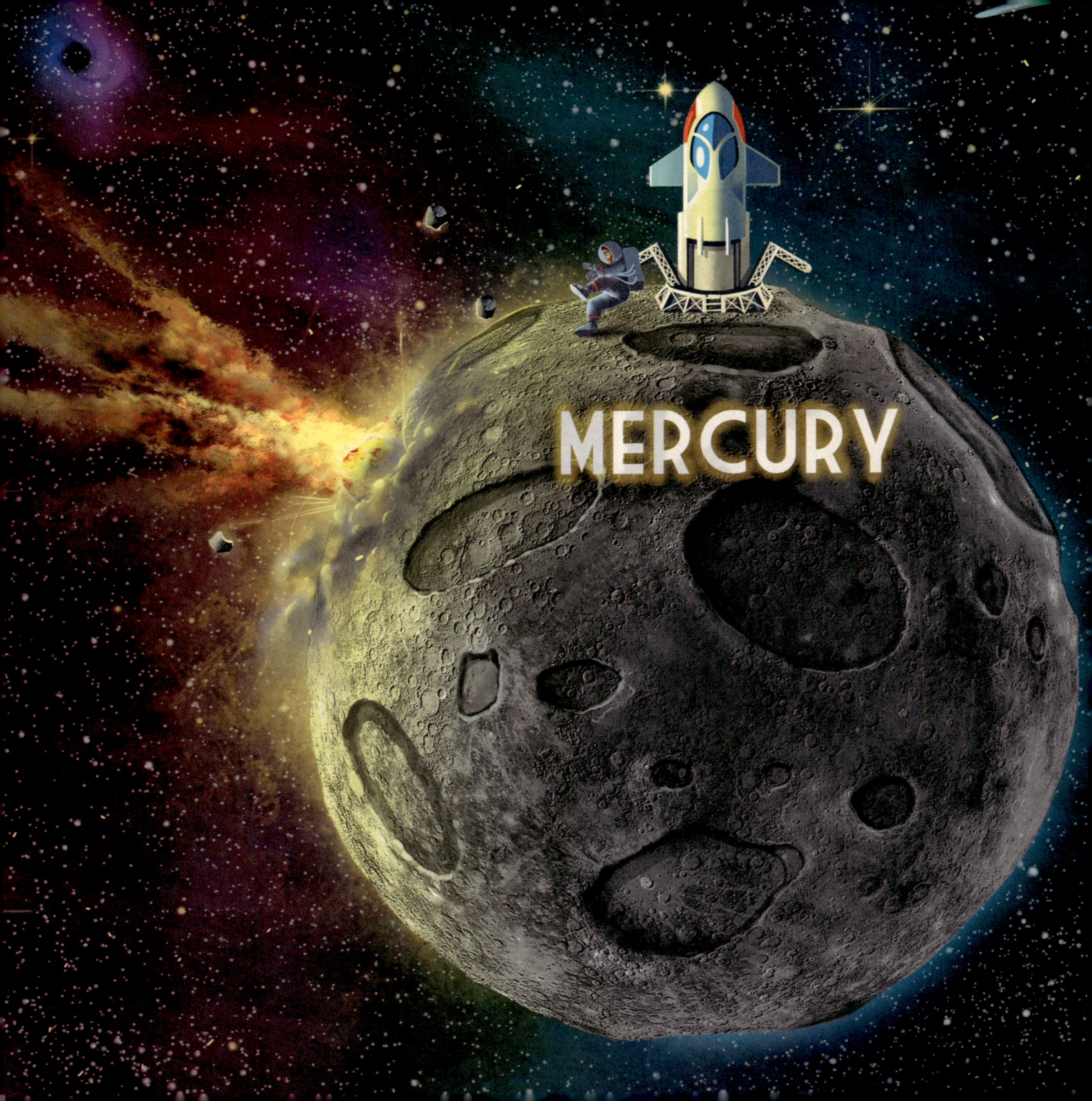

VENUS

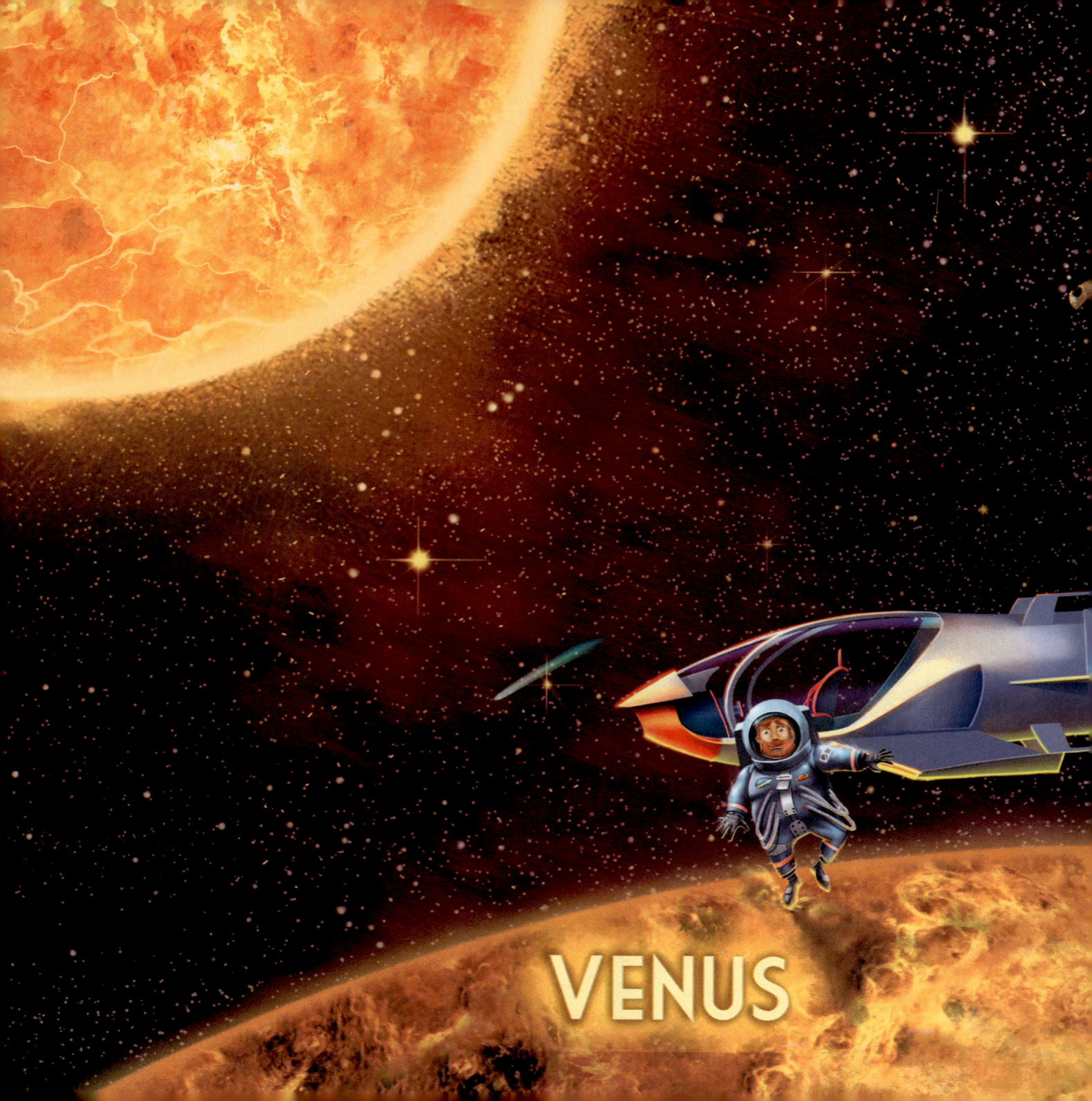

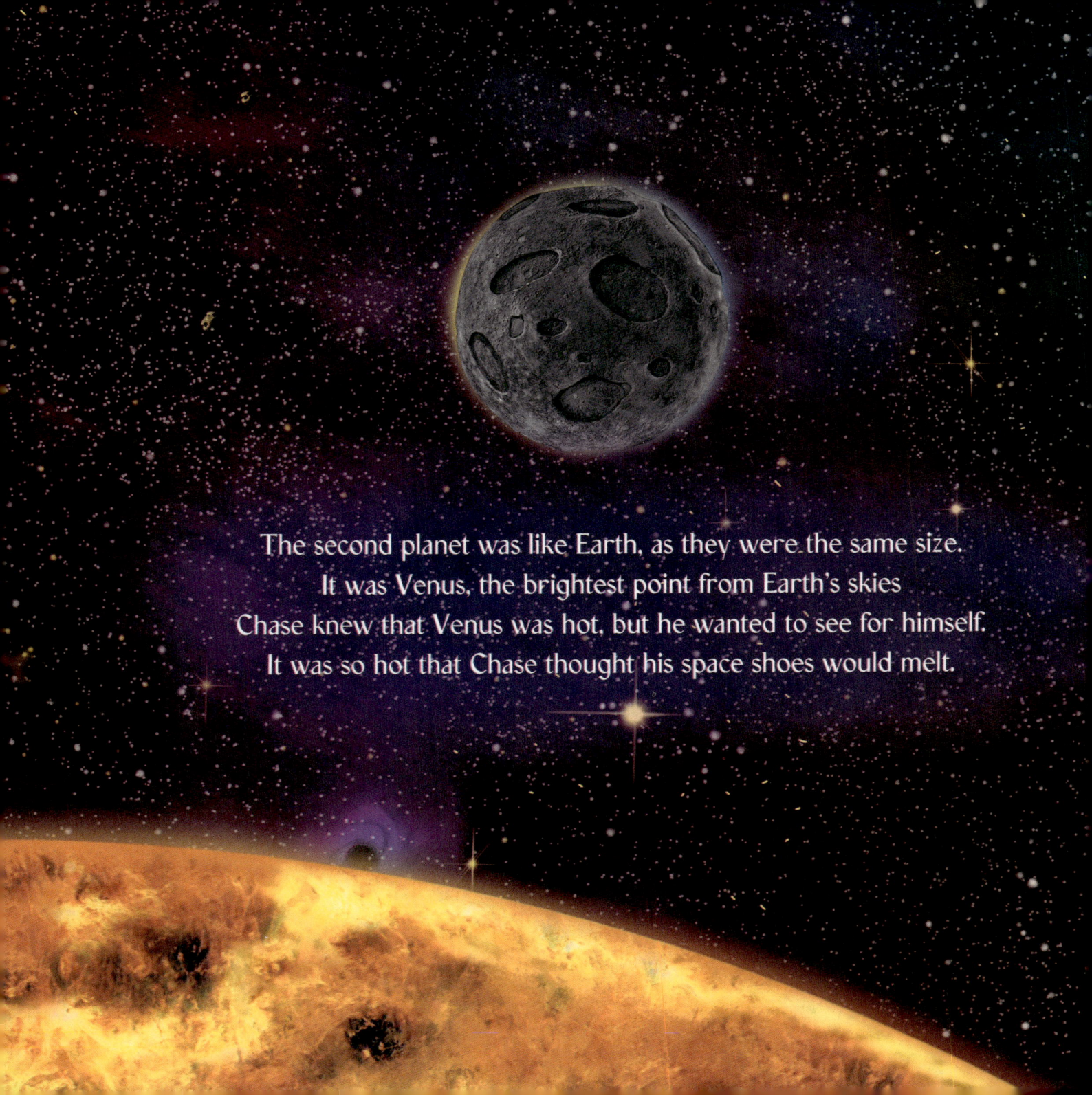

The second planet was like Earth, as they were the same size.
It was Venus, the brightest point from Earth's skies
Chase knew that Venus was hot, but he wanted to see for himself.
It was so hot that Chase thought his space shoes would melt.

Chase came upon Earth, the planet from which he first arrived.
He looked at the green land and blue color of the water and sky.
The Earth is covered in water about 70 percent
Now Chase could see for himself exactly what that meant

EARTH

INTERNATIONAL SPACE STATION

Our cosmic friend Chase wanted to learn so much more.
He went to the International Space Station for a little tour.
Here he discovered a science lab and found out things he did not know.
Like how space affects our lives and if it's going to rain or snow.

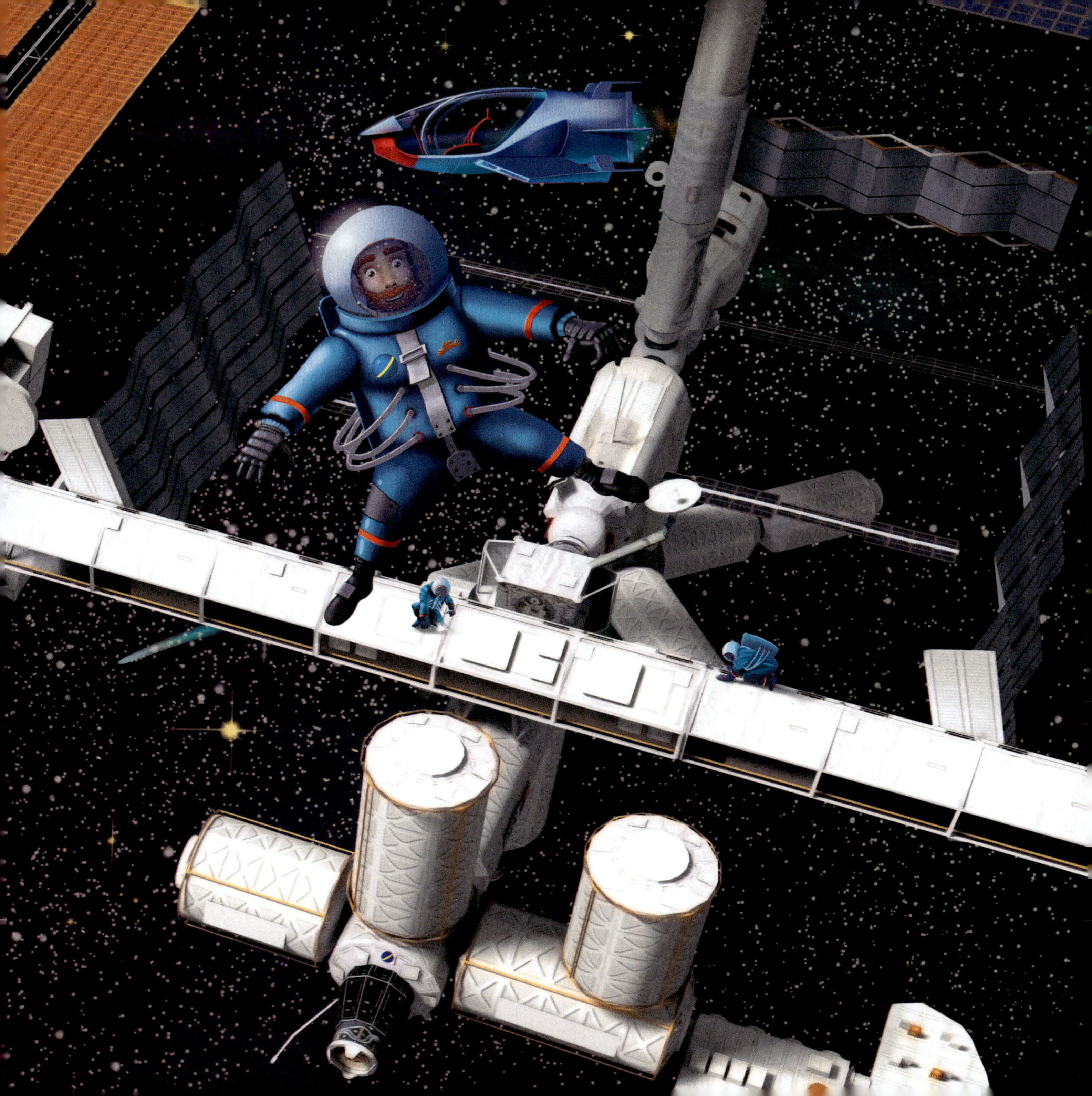

Near the Earth, Chase saw a small circle that turned out to be the moon.
He walked around and found the U.S. flag standing up within a dune.
Americans were the first ones to walk on the moon's floor.
Now a lunar rover roams the surface so we can always see more.

MOON

The moon is quite different because it is not a planet or a star.
However, the moon hovers the Earth, which can be seen from afar.
Chase remembered the nights he stared up into the cosmic sky.
He always imagined going up there and giving the moonwalk a try.

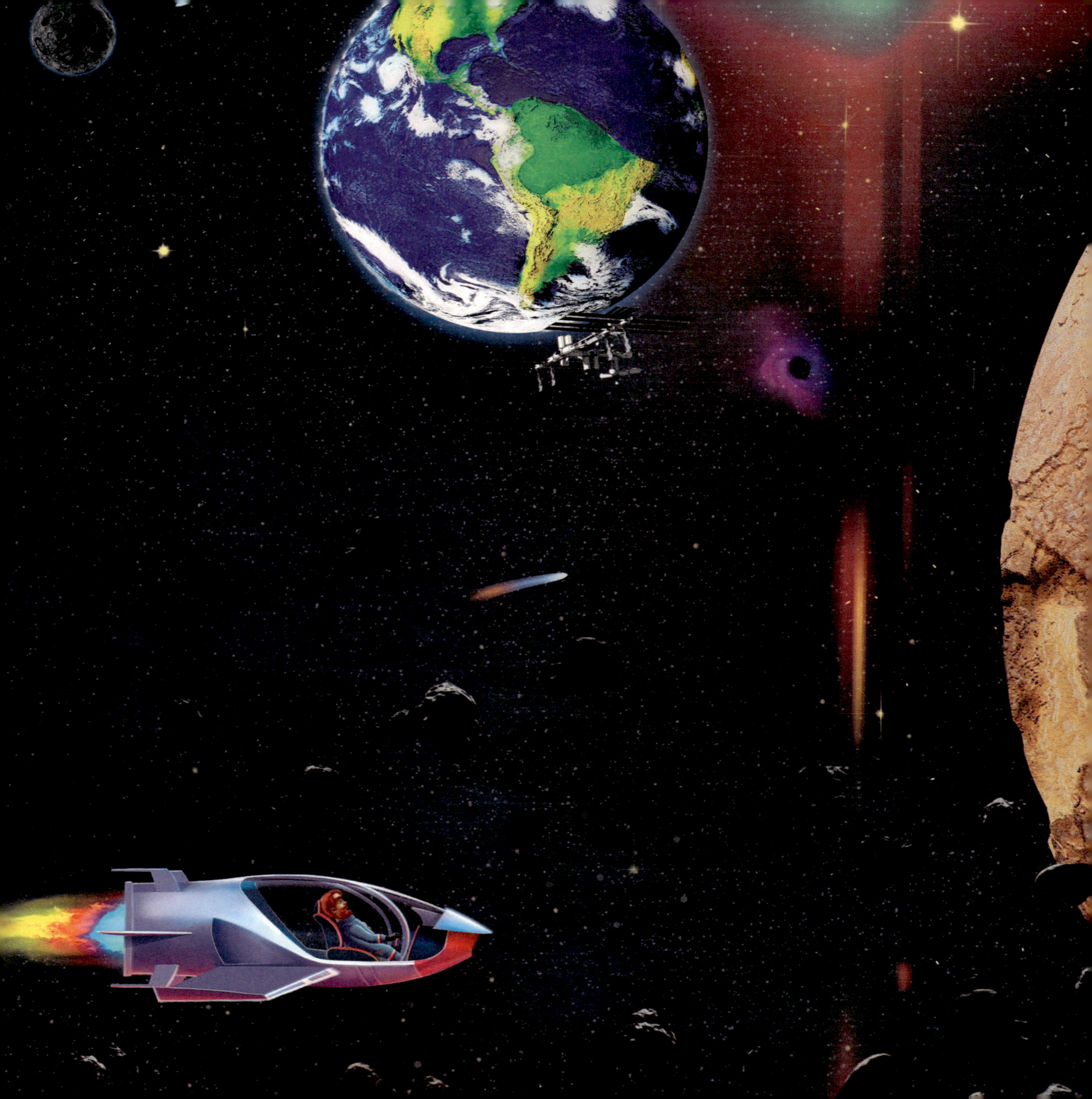

After leaving the moon, Chase flew towards a planet that appeared red.
The Red Planet was Mars, and it contained red stones instead.
Chase ran into a few comets on the way, but he made it through.
He decided to land on Mars and explore for a minute or two.

MARS

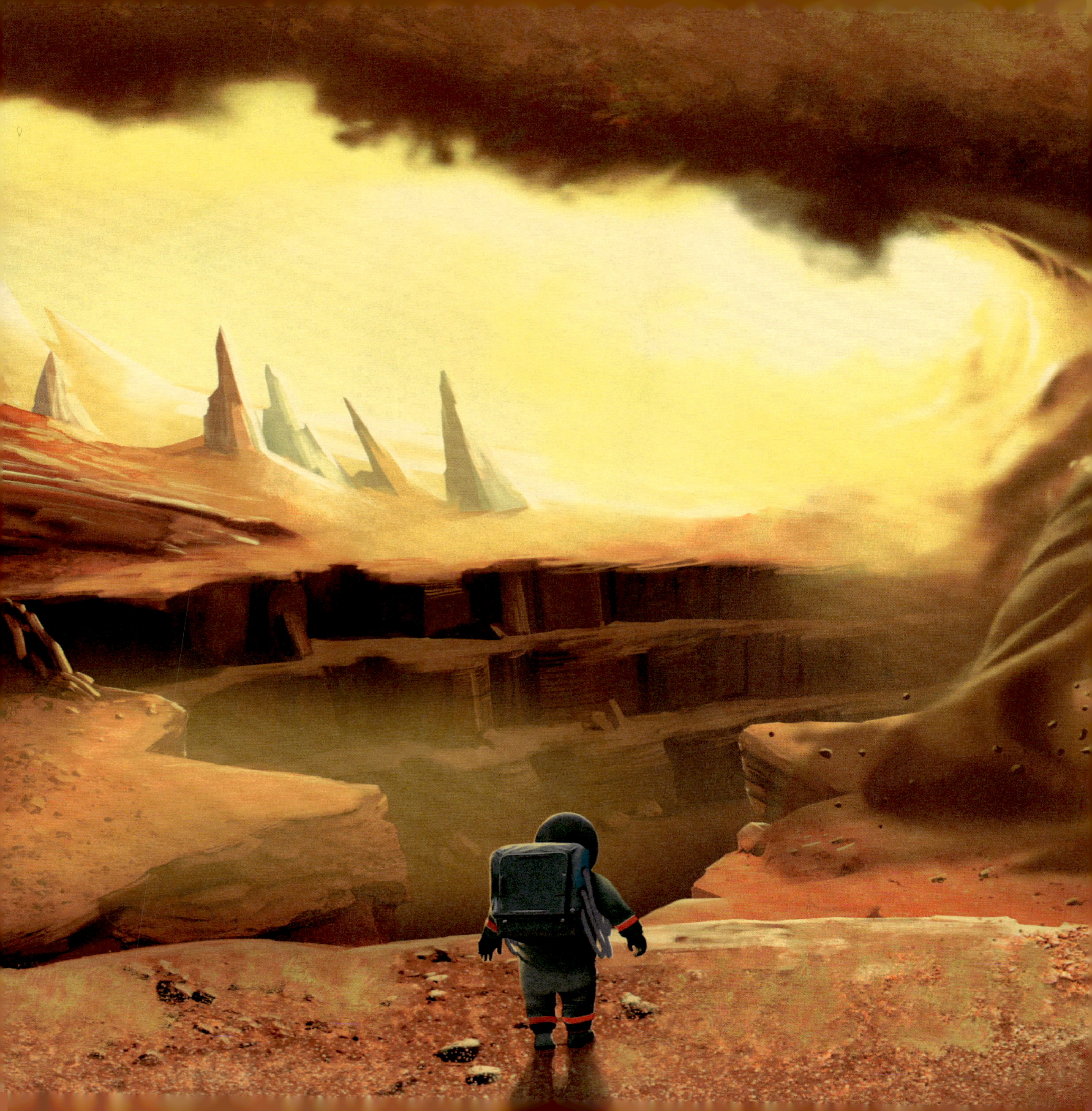

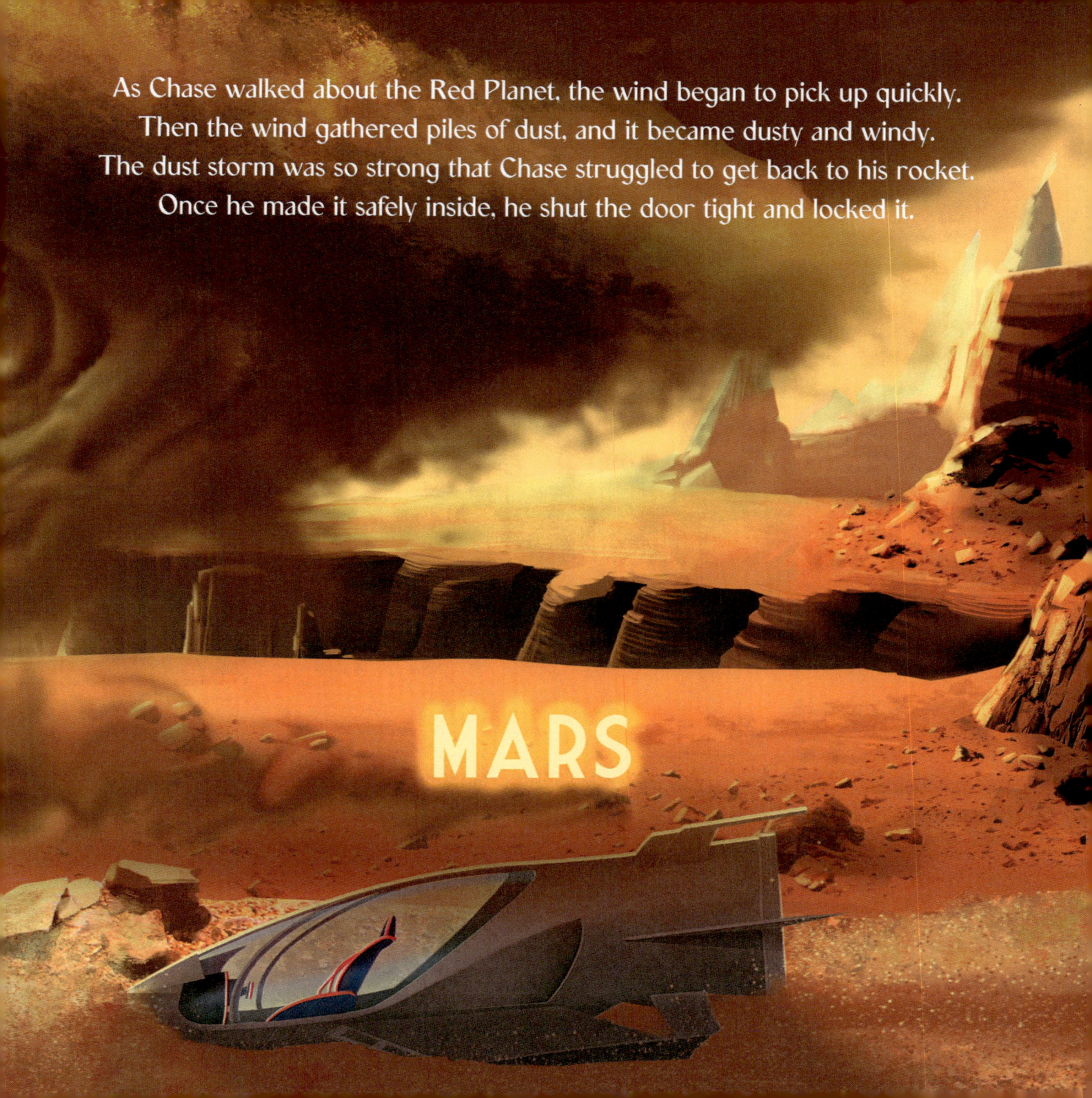

As Chase walked about the Red Planet, the wind began to pick up quickly.
Then the wind gathered piles of dust, and it became dusty and windy.
The dust storm was so strong that Chase struggled to get back to his rocket.
Once he made it safely inside, he shut the door tight and locked it.

MARS

Chase then made it to Jupiter, the fifth planet from the sun.
Jupiter was very large, but in size, it is not number one.
Jupiter is special because it protects our Earth from comets falling in.
It attracts the comets to itself, making it Earth's best planet friend.

JUPITER

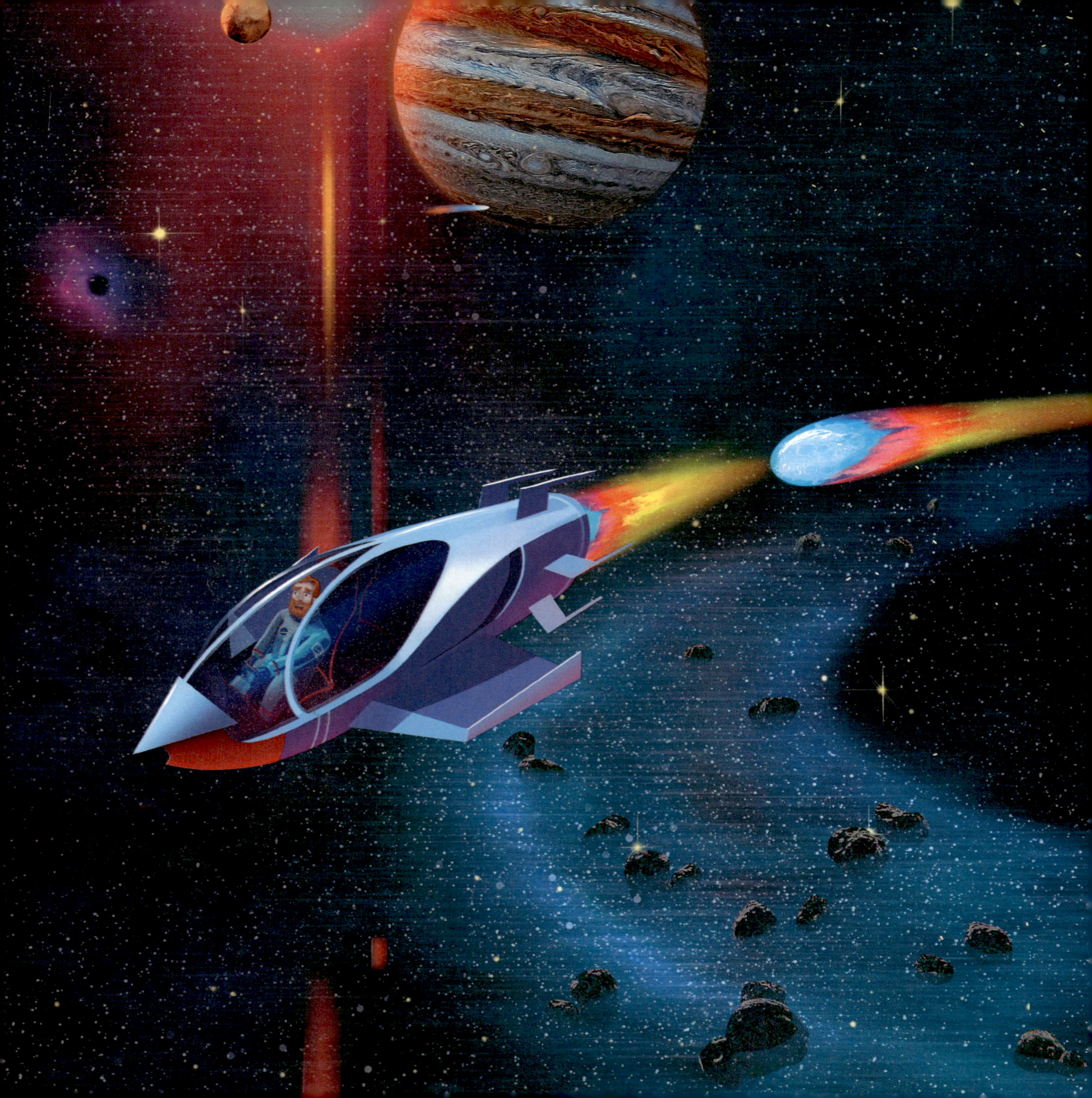

SATURN

The next planet was Saturn, smaller than the planet before
Saturn has beautiful rings which is what it is known for.
Chase could not land on Saturn because it is made up of gas.
He looked at the planet as a comet suddenly shot by fast.

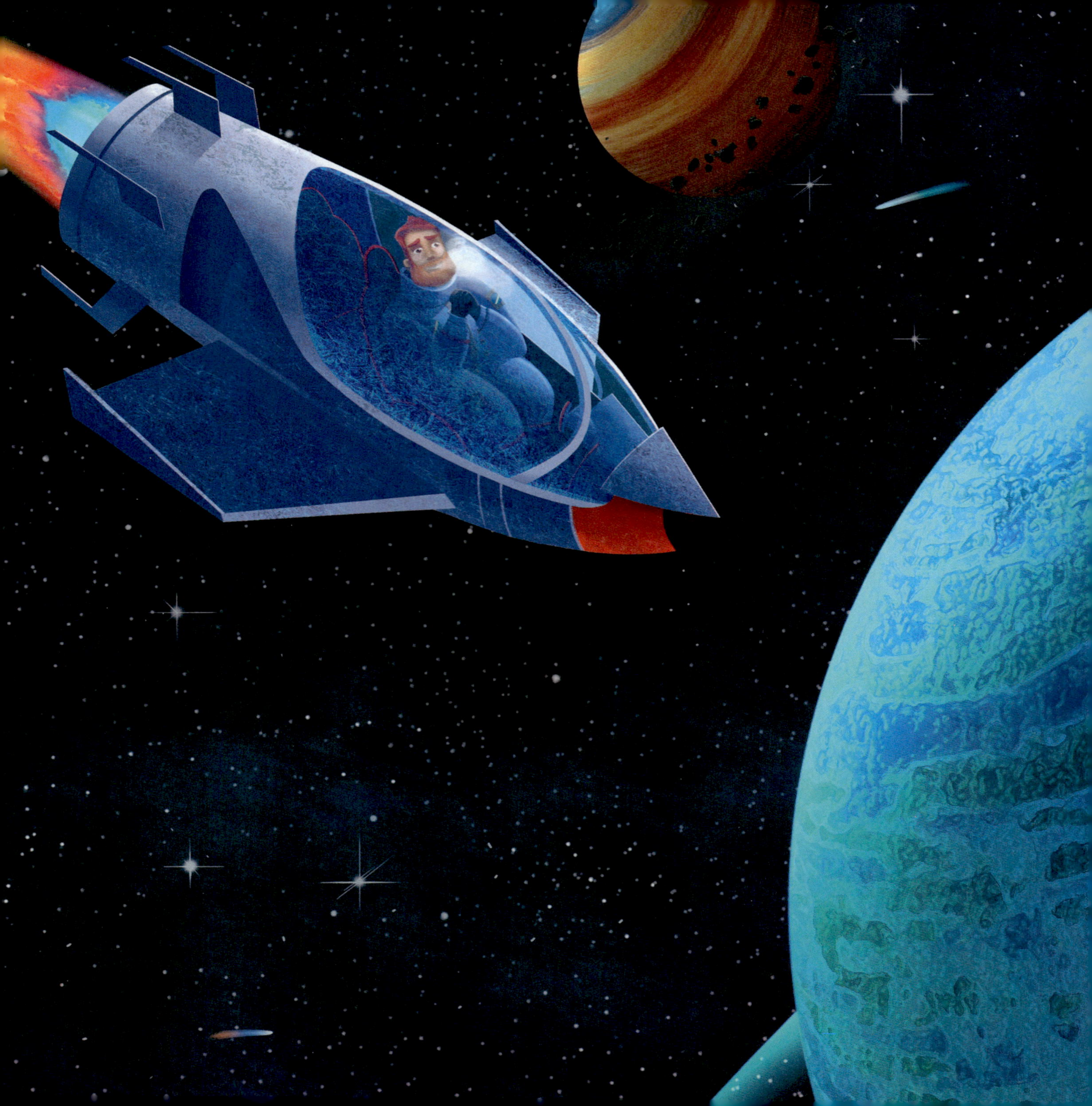

URANUS

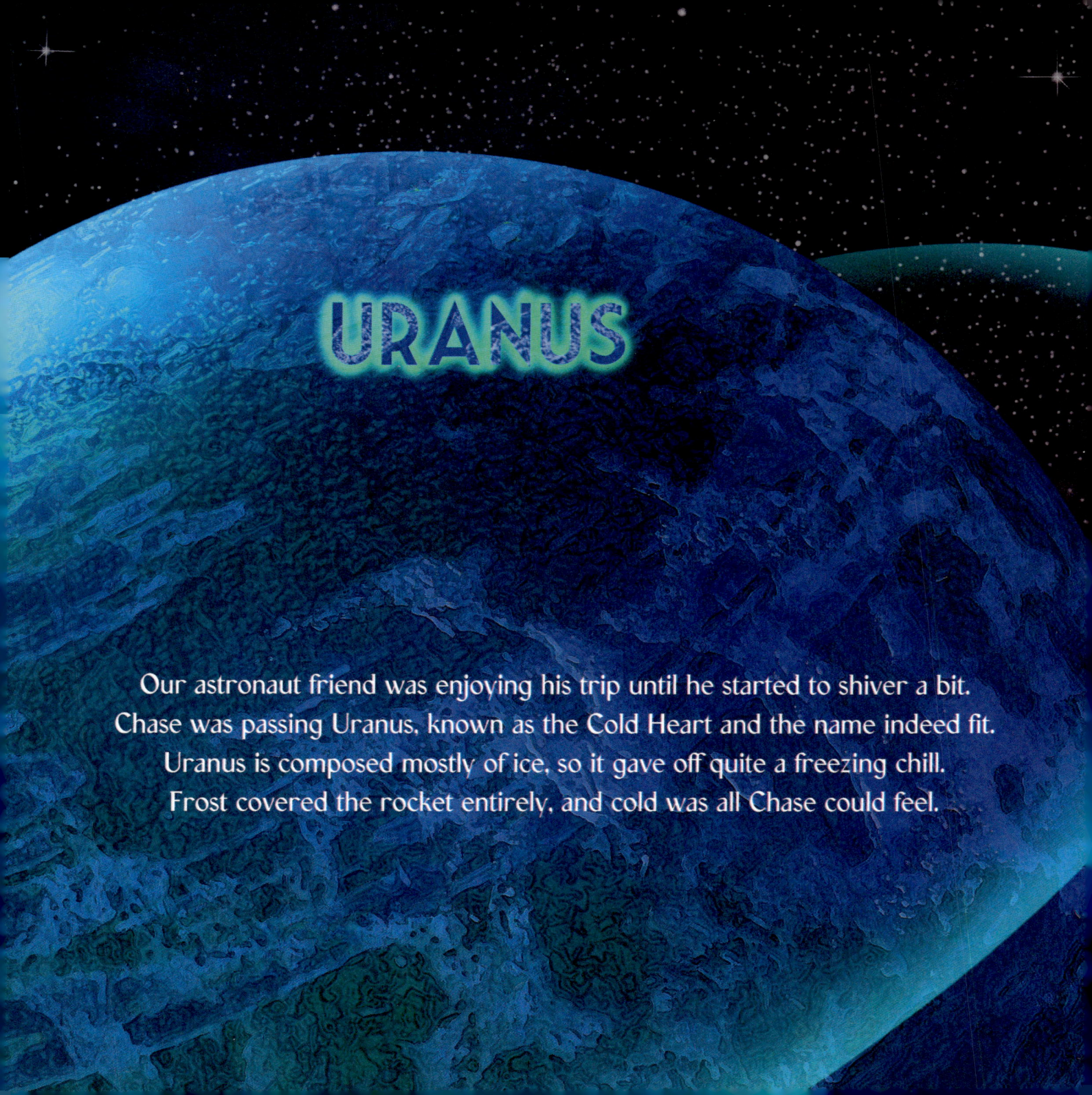

Our astronaut friend was enjoying his trip until he started to shiver a bit.
Chase was passing Uranus, known as the Cold Heart and the name indeed fit.
Uranus is composed mostly of ice, so it gave off quite a freezing chill.
Frost covered the rocket entirely, and cold was all Chase could feel.

Chase finally arrived at the planet Neptune after a very long journey.
Neptune gets its name from mythology, after the Roman God of the Sea.
It is the farthest planet from the sun, so it is dark and very cold.
Chase could not stop and land because the planet would not hold.

Chase thought that Uranus was cold but Neptune was freezing
The cold air damaged his rocket which was not very pleasing
He had to go out in the chilly space air to repair his rocket
Chase used an astronaut tool that he kept inside his pocket

NEPTUNE

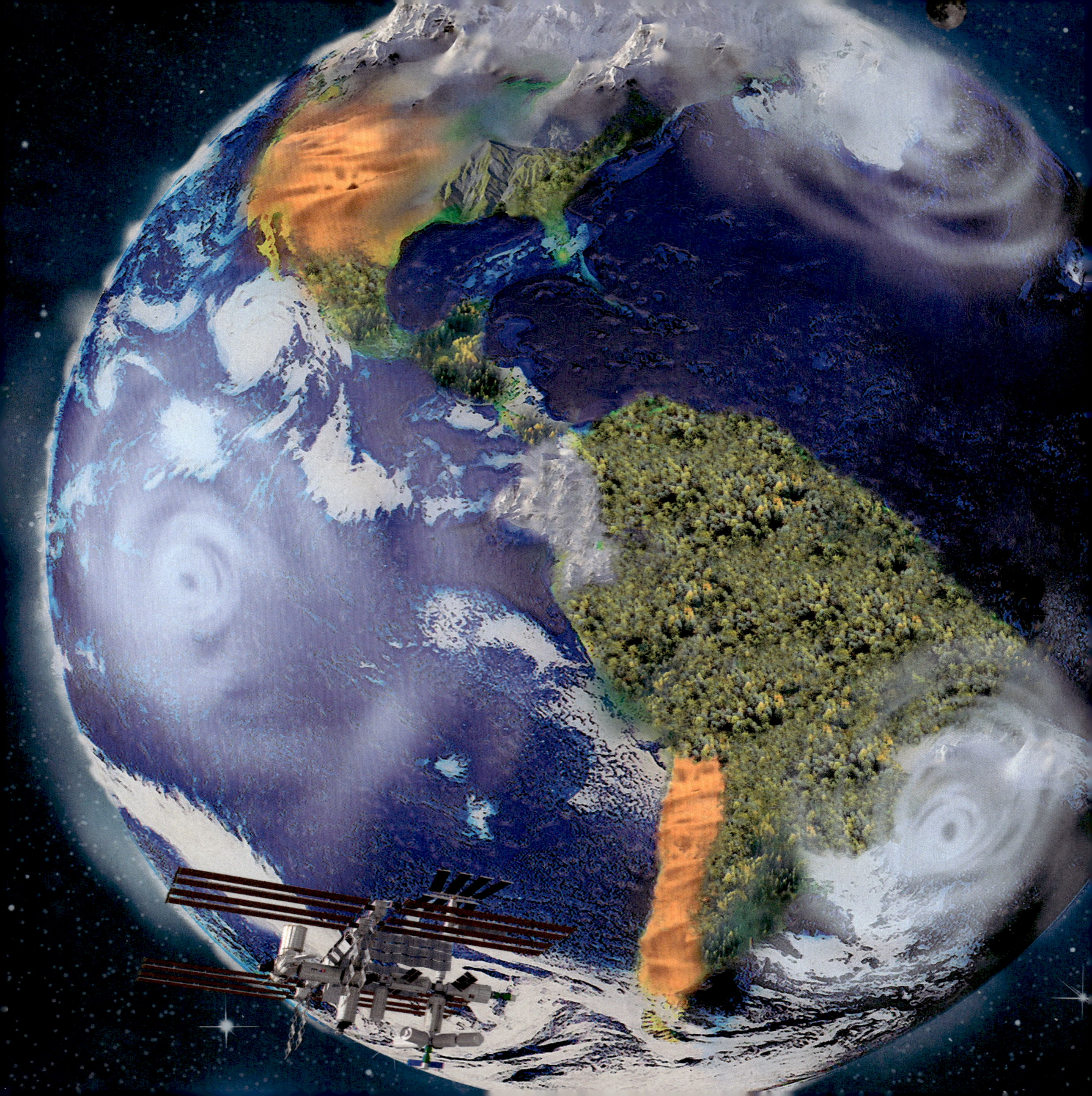

The young space explorer made his way through the galaxy to go home.
He passed by all the planets in the solar system he had known.
He flew by the International Space Station and its gadgets that predict the weather.
Chase knew that because of those gadgets, people could plan things better.

After an out-of-this-world adventure, Chase landed at the rocket station.
He parked his rocket next to the other ones for an examination.
He had quite a long day and was finally ready to go to bed.
Although all the planets he saw still lingered in his head.

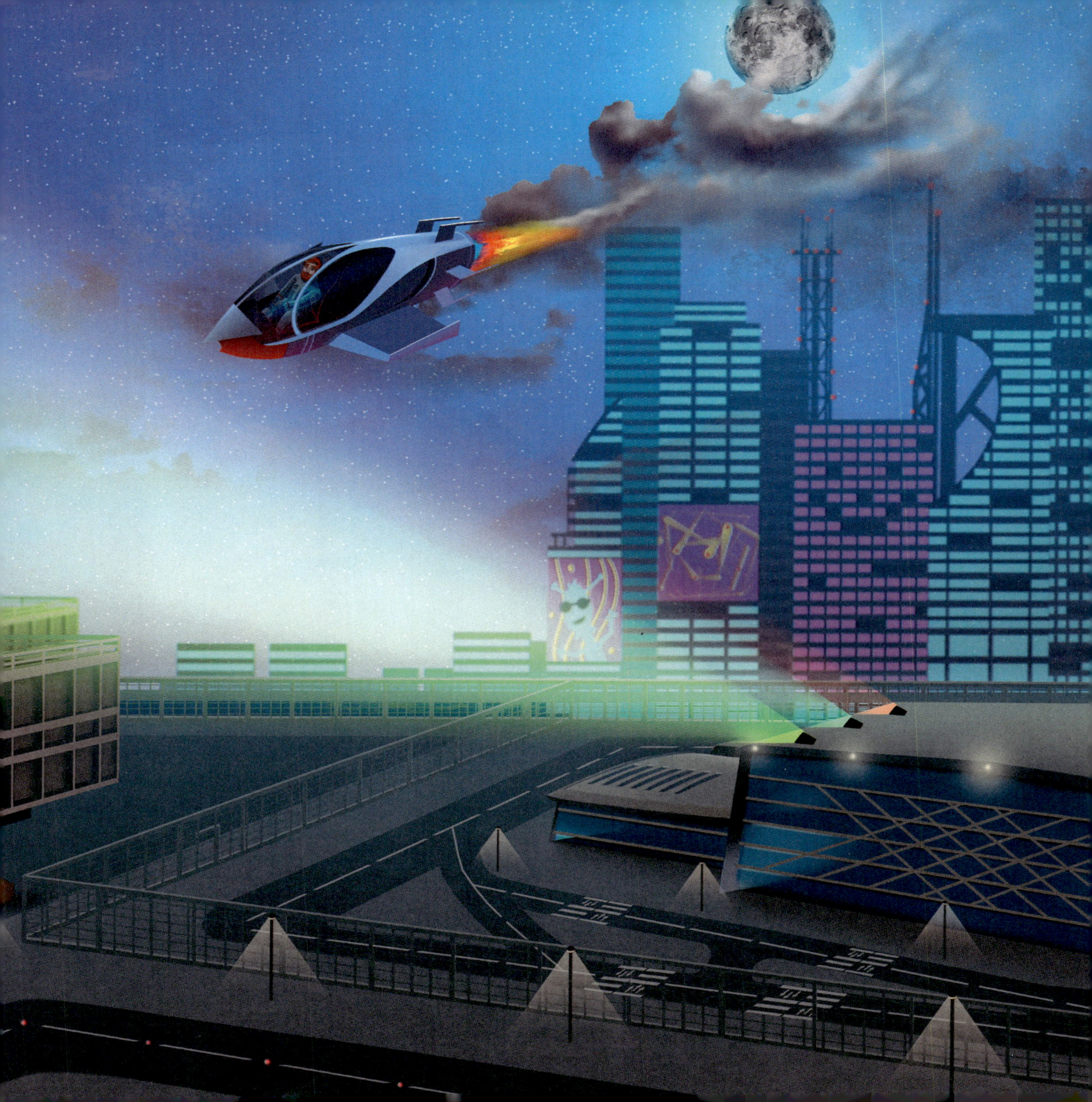

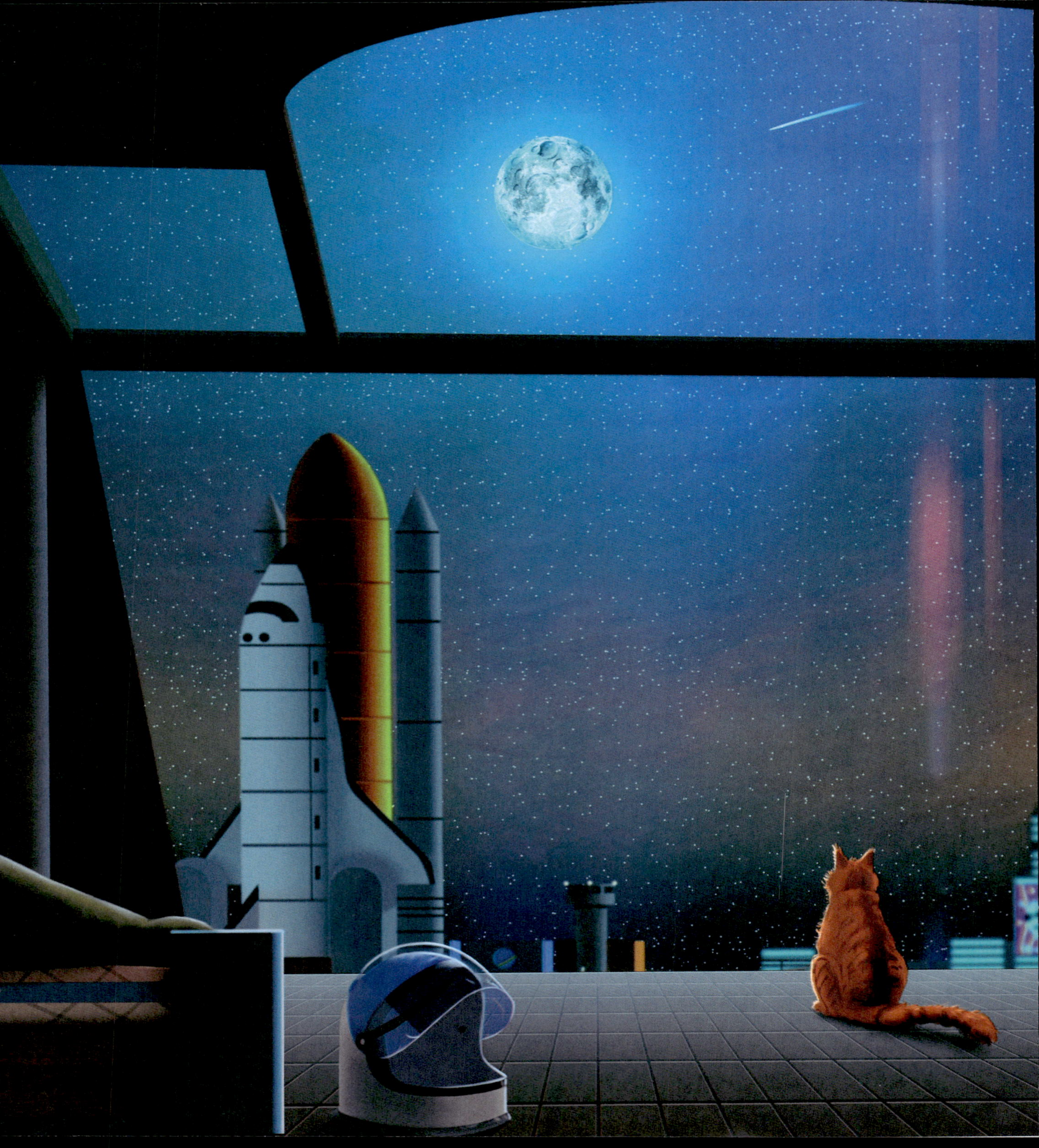

When Chase laid down, he looked up into the starlit sky.
He thought about how awesome it was that he was up so high.
Chase was exhausted after such a fascinating time in outer space.
Then he fell soundly asleep as the moonlight hit his face.

Good Night

Made in the USA
Middletown, DE
16 April 2021